Orkney & Shetland Steamers

ALISTAIR DEAYTON

ORKNEY & SHETLAND STEAMERS

ALISTAIR DEAYTON

TEMPUS

First published 2002
Copyright © Alistair Deayton, 2002

PUBLISHED IN THE UNITED KINGDOM BY:

Tempus Publishing Ltd
The Mill, Brimscombe Port
Stroud, Gloucestershire GL5 2QG
www.tempus-publishing.com

PUBLISHED IN THE UNITED STATES OF AMERICA BY:

Tempus Publishing Inc.
2 Cumberland Street
Charleston, SC 29401
(Tel: 1-888-313-2665)
www.tempuspublishing.com
ISBN 0 7524 2377 0

Typesetting and origination by
Tempus Publishing Limited
Printed in Great Britain by
Midway Colour Print, Wiltshire

Contents

Acknowledgements

The majority of the photographs in this book come from the collection of the late Alastair McRobb, acknowledged expert on the North Company. My thanks go to his widow, Mrs Maureen McRobb, for permission to use these.

My thanks go to Alastair Cormack for illustration on Orkney local steamers, for the use of the map on page 110, and for help on the history of Orkney vessels in the thirty years; to Bård Kolltveit for photographs of North Company steamers in Norway; to Malcolm McRonald for the illustrations of St Clair relieving at Liverpool; and also to Iain Quinn and Ian Somerville.

Several publications on the North Company have been invaluable, notably Northwards by Sea by Professor Gordon Donaldson, The North Boats by Alastair W. McRobb and Days of Orkney Steam by Alastair and Anne Cormack.

My thanks also go to Alastair and Anne Cormack and to Ian Somerville for checking the text for errors.

Introduction

The replacement of P&O Scottish Ferries by Northlink as the ferry company serving Orkney and Shetland in October 2002 will bring to an end an unbroken line of ownership that stretches back to the dawn of steam navigation and before. The North of Scotland, Orkney & Shetland Steam Navigation Co., known as the North Company, operated from 1875 for a century, albeit with the name altered to North of Scotland, Orkney & Shetland Shipping Co. Ltd from 1953, until, as part of the P&O group, it was renamed P&O Ferries (Orkney & Shetland). The story started in 1790 when a company named the Leith & Clyde Shipping Co. was formed to operate sailing vessels between Leith and the Clyde. In 1820 this company amalgamated with the Aberdeen, Dundee & Leith Shipping Co. to form the Aberdeen, Leith, Clyde & Tay Shipping Co., and from 1824 this was known as the Aberdeen, Leith & Clyde Shipping Co.

Services were operated by sailing smacks until the first steamer, *Velocity* of 1821, entered service, which operated from Aberdeen to Leith with about seven intermediate stops. Initially, steamers were replaced by sailing smacks during the winter months. In 1826 *Brilliant*, operated by the competing Leith & Aberdeen Steam Yacht Co., was purchased, operating to Inverness and regular services from Aberdeen to Wick and Kirkwall were started from 1833. In 1839 *Sovereign* was introduced and the frequency of the Wick and Kirkwall service was increased to weekly with a fortnightly extension to Lerwick, a route not dissimilar to that of today's *St Sunniva*. Various other paddle steamers were introduced and some lost or sold over the next twenty years. Around 1840/1841 Granton replaced Newhaven as the Edinburgh terminal and, in 1850, a new route to Wick and Scrabster commenced. This new Caithness service meant that the calls at Wick by the Kirkwall and Lerwick steamer were dropped.

In 1861 the company had its first screw steamer built, *Queen (II)*. She was an all-the-year round steamer, enabling the last of the sailing vessels, *Fairy*, to be withdrawn from the winter Lerwick service. In 1866 a second weekly service to Kirkwall and Lerwick was added, initially operated by *Queen*, and was known as the secondary indirect route. 1867 saw the purchase of the company's final paddle steamer, the North British Railway's *Waverley* from the Silloth to Dublin route. She was renamed *St Magnus*, commencing a style of nomenclature that has lasted into the twenty-first century. In the following year she was joined by *St Clair (I)*, which was to last for sixty-nine years. In 1871 *St Nicholas* joined the fleet, and was placed on the Caithness service.

From 1861 Stornoway was served as an extension of the Caithness service during the Herring season of May/June. In 1881 a west-side service was introduced to Stromness and Scalloway, with a number of other calls to isolated communities on the west side of Shetland, including Hillswick where the company had the St Magnus Hotel built in 1900. In 1882 the North Company took over the Pentland Firth service from Scrabster to Scapa pier and Stromness. The steamer *St Olaf* was built in that year for this service, but had a short life with the company. She was sold in 1890 and replaced by *St Ola* in 1892.

1883 saw the building of the first steamer over 1,000 gross tons, *St Rognvald (I)*. In 1886 she introduced Norwegian cruises. *St Sunniva (I)* was built to join her on these cruises in 1887, and was the first purpose-built cruise steamer in the world.

In 1890 the Shetland Island Steam Navigation Co., was wholly taken over, having previously been 50% owned by the North Company. Their *Earl of Zetland* had been built in 1877 and served the north isles of Shetland from Lerwick for almost seventy years.

In the following year *St Nicholas* introduced a twice-weekly direct Aberdeen to Lerwick service. In 1895 *St Ninian (I)* was built, and the fleet now stood at ten. On 24 April 1900, *St Rognvald* ran aground in fog on Stronsay. In 1901 a replacement was built, taking her predecessor's name, and also replacing the last surviving paddle steamer, the *St Magnus*.

In 1908 the Norwegian cruises were withdrawn and *St Sunniva* converted to a mail steamer, operating on the direct route from Aberdeen to Lerwick.

The First World War saw the loss of three steamers: newly purchased *Express* in April 1917, off the French coast; *St Margaret* in September of the same year, torpedoed 30 miles east of the Faeroes en route from Lerwick to Iceland; and *St Magnus (II)*, due to enemy action off Peterhead on 19 January 1918.

In 1919 MacBrayne's *Chieftain* was purchased and became *St Margaret (II)*, and in 1924 the newly built *St Magnus (III)* joined the fleet. In April 1930 the *St Sunniva* was lost after running aground on Mousa. A second *St Sunniva* was built, arguably the most beautiful coastal liner ever built, with a white hull, yacht-like looks and a clipper bow. In 1936 the *St Clair* was renamed *St Colm*, to release her name for a new steamer, slightly larger than *St Magnus*.

August 1939 saw the first motorship in the fleet, *Earl of Zetland (II)*. After little over a week she was requisitioned by the Admiralty and her predecessor continued to maintain the North Isles services for a further six years. A number of other steamers were requisitioned in the Second World War. Four steamers were losses during the war: cargo steamer *St Fergus* following a collision and *St Catherine* by bombing, both in 1940; cargo steamer *St Clement* by bombing in 1941; and *St Sunniva*, which was lost with all hands while serving as a rescue ship with a northern convoy in January 1943. It is believed she capsized after being iced over.

A post-war new building programme saw three motorships built for the North Company: cargo ship *St Clement* in 1946, *St Ninian* for the indirect route in 1950, and *St Ola (II)* for the Pentland Firth service in 1951. *St Rognvald (III)* entered the fleet in 1955; she was originally to have space for fifty passengers, but she entered service as a twelve-passenger vessel. The replacement of older steamers saw *St Clair (III)* enter the fleet in 1960 on the direct route from Aberdeen to Lerwick. She was the last non-vehicle carrying vessel to be built for the fleet.

The car ferry age started in February 1975 when *St Ola (III)* was built for the Scrabster to Stromness service. A month later *Earl of Zetland* was withdrawn, having been replaced by five small car ferries owned by Zetland County Council.

Coast Lines Ltd had taken over the North Company in 1961, and were themselves taken over by the P&O group a decade later. In October 1975 the North Company name was replaced by that of P&O Ferries.

In April 1977, *St Clair (IV)* entered service, formerly *SF Panther*, operating on P&O Ferries Southern Ferries service from Southampton to northern Spain. In 1987 another Panther, this time *NF Panther* from P&O Normandy Ferries' Dover to Boulogne service, came into service as the third *St Sunniva*, reopening the indirect passenger service from

Aberdeen to Lerwick, now via Stromness rather than Kirkwall. This enabled mini-cruises to be offered including calls at both Orkney and Shetland. From 1989 the operator has been known as P&O Scottish Ferries.

In 1992 both St Ola and St Clair were replaced, their replacements continuing with the same name. From 1993 to 1997 St Clair made a summer-only weekly run from Lerwick to Bergen.

The services to Orkney and Shetland were put out to tender in the late nineties and the tender was won by P&O Scottish Ferries in 1997. A further tender, to start in 2002, was won by a consortium of Caledonian MacBrayne and the Royal Bank of Scotland known as Northlink Orkney & Shetland Ferries Ltd. Three new vessels have been ordered, one, Hamnavoe for the Scrabster to Stromness service, two passenger ferries, Hjaltland and Hrossey to serve Lerwick direct and via Kirkwall, while a freight ferry, Hascosay, has been purchased second-hand.

Competitors

There has been very little competition to the North Company over the years.

In 1860 the former Isle of Man Steam Packet Co. paddle steamer Ben My Chree was advertised to sail from Granton and Aberdeen to Invergordon and Inverness.

From 1903 to 1907 the Shetland Isles Steam Trading Co., owned by Sandisons, a firm of general merchants in Unst and Yell, provided a service from Aberdeen to Lerwick and the North Isles, initially using the chartered Mona, then Trojan, also chartered, and finally the only steamer owned by that company, Norseman. The latter reportedly foundered on a delivery voyage to new owners in South America.

A passenger-only service from Burwick to John O'Groats has been maintained since the 1970s, initially with the launch Pentalina, then with Souters Lass, and since 1987 with Pentland Venture. These services have bus connections from Inverness and Kirkwall. A company named Orkney Ferries commenced a car ferry route with Varagen from Burwick to Gills Bay, west of John O'Groats in 1989, but the link span at Gills Bay was washed away in a storm and the route did not survive. In 2001, Pentland Ferries re-opened the route, this time from St Margaret's Hope with Pentalina B, formerly Caledonian MacBrayne's Iona.

In 1986, Syllingar, ex-Scillonian, briefly operated a service from Kirkwall to Scalloway for Norse Atlantic Ferries.

Orkney Local Steamers

Services from Kirkwall to the principal North Isles except Shapinsay were maintained by the Orkney Steam Navigation Co. from 1868 until 1961, and since then by the Orkney Islands Shipping Co. Ltd, taken over by Orkney Islands Council in 1987, more recently trading as Orkney Ferries. Orcadia maintained the service from 1868 until 1931. The two 'Steam Earls', Earl Thorfinn of 1928 and Earl Sigurd of 1931 operated until 1963 and 1969 respectively. The motor vessel Orcadia replaced them in 1962, and Islander in 1969, and these two carried on until the car ferry earls, Earl Thorfinn and Earl Sigurd, came into service in 1990. They were joined the following year by Varagen, which had been built for the abortive Pentland Firth service.

Services to the south Isles of Hoy, Graemsay, Flotta and, prior to the construction of the Churchill Barriers, Burray and South Ronaldsay, were maintained by the steamer Hoy Head of 1896 under various owners until the formation of Bremner & Co. of Stromness in 1938. They had a number of other vessels and coasters, some serving the admiralty establishments in Scapa Flow, operating until 1974 when they were taken over by the Orkney Islands Shipping Co. William Dennison of Shapinsay operated a number of vessels on the route from Kirkwall to that island from 1914 until 1968.

EXCURSION TRIP

BY SEA.

WICK TO LOSSIEMOUTH

AND BACK.

S.S. 'ST. CLAIR'

IS INTENDED TO LEAVE WICK ON

WEDNESDAY, 25TH JUNE

AT 7 A.M., FOR LOSSIEMOUTH,

ARRIVING THERE ABOUT 11 A.M. WHERE THE EXCURSIONISTS WILL BE LANDED.

THE RETURN PASSAGE WILL BE FROM LOSSIEMOUTH AT 7 P.M.

ARRIVING AT WICK ABOUT 11 P.M.

RETURN PASSAGE FARES . FIRST CABIN, **11/6**; SECOND CABIN, **7/-**
THE RETURN RAILWAY FARE BETWEEN LOSSIEMOUTH AND ELGIN IS 6d.

Tickets may be had at the Office --- Harbour Quay, Wick.

BY ORDER,

JAMES McCALLUM, Manager.

J. HENDERSON, PRINTER, WICK.

On at least one occasion, such as on Wednesday 25 June 1930, *St Clair (I)* offered a day excursion from Wick to Lossiemouth.

One

North Company Steamers of the Nineteenth Century

Sovereign was typical of the early North Company paddle steamers. Built in 1836 by John Wood of Port Glasgow with engines by Robert Napier, she was the third steamer in the fleet, and inaugurated the Lerwick service in the summer of that year. In 1859 she appears to have run on charter to the Aberdeen Steam Navigation Co. from Aberdeen to Inverness, and from 1860 until her withdrawal in the following year she ran from Aberdeen to Wick. After being sold in 1865 she had a succession of owners, and in 1872 ran aground on Arklow Bank. After being refloated, she ran as a sailing ship until wrecked at Muros, in Spain, in 1901. She is seen here entering Aberdeen Harbour, in a painting attributed to Arthur Smith. (*Aberdeen Art Gallery & Museum*)

ST. MAGNUS HOTEL · HILLSWICK

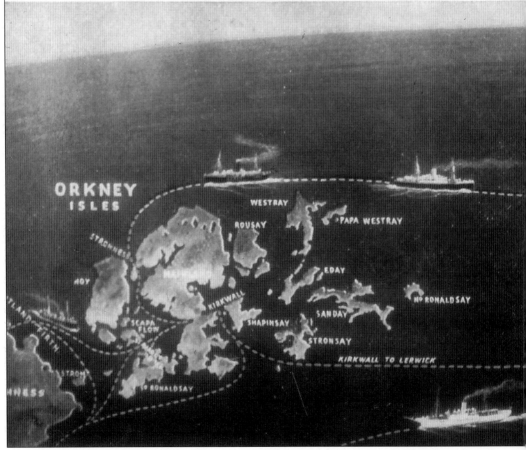

A map of Orkney and Shetland from a 1938 brochure. Note *St Sunniva (II)* at the foot on the Aberdeen to Lerwick service, and the west side service to Stromness and Scalloway,

R.M.S. "ST. SUNNIVA"

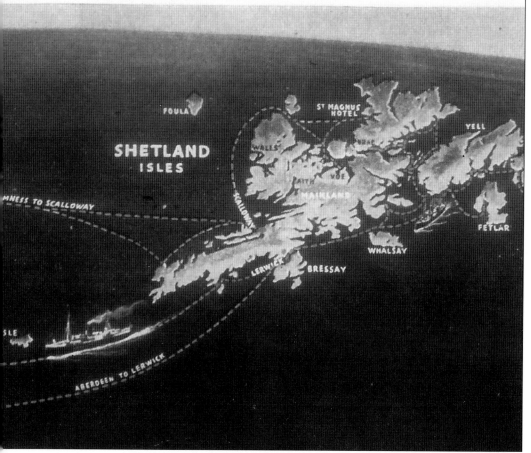

continuing in a triangle to Voe and the St Magnus Hotel at Hillswick.

Queen (II) was built by Smith & Rodger at Port Glasgow in 1861 with compound machinery by J. Howden. She was the first screw steamer in the fleet and initially served on the Caithness route in summer, and after 1866 took on the second summer service to Shetland. In 1881 she pioneered the west coast service. She was sold to Turkish owners in 1911, renamed *Amalia*, and was seized at Sevastopol in 1917 during the Russian Revolution, and broken up. She is seen here at Lerwick.

St Magnus (I) had been built in 1864 as *Waverley* for the Silloth to Dublin service of the North British Steam Packet Co., which was owned by North British Railway. C. Mitchell of Walker-on-Tyne built her with engines by Robert Stephenson & Co., and it is reputed that she was originally built as a blockade-runner for the US Civil War. Her machinery was troublesome and she saw less than a month's service from Silloth. In 1866 she returned to the Tyne and her engine troubles were resolved. In 1867 she was sold to the North Company and renamed *St Magnus*. She is seen here at Lerwick.

Deck saloon of *St Magnus (I)*. In her time with the North Company she operated from Leith and Aberdeen to Kirkwall and Lerwick, on either the secondary indirect service or the weekend service.

A detail shot of *St Magnus (I)* at Aberdeen.

St Magnus (I) towards the end of her career at Kirkwall, taken from a hotel window. She was sold in 1904 to Gibraltar owners and broken up at Rotterdam in 1913.

St Clair (I) was built in 1868 by Randolph Elder & Co. at Govan. She served on the summer Caithness service to Wick for most of her career, and is seen here entering Wick Harbour in a postcard view.

St Clair (I) in another view, also arriving at Wick, with unidentified Langlands & Hain Line steamers in the background.

The damaged bow of *St Clair (I)* after an unknown collision, 29 August 1914.

STROMNESS & WEST MAINLAND HOLIDAY
THURSDAY, 5TH JULY
EXCURSION
To THURSO

THE S.S. 'ST. CLAIR'

(Weather permitting)

Will leave STROMNESS at 8 a.m. for SCRABSTER
Returning from Scrabster at 6 p.m.

FARES:—First Cabin, 10s; Second Cabin, 6s.
Children under 14 years, Half-fare.
Tickets will be issued at the Steamer's Office, Stromness.

Motor Tours to John O' Groats and Wick can be arranged.
For particulars apply to JOHN M. SLATER, Agent.

JAMES MᶜCALLUM, Manager.

Aberdeen, 14th June 1928.

St Clair (I) offered day trips from Scapa Pier to Thurso on the annual Stromness and West Mainland Holiday, advertised in this poster from 1928.

EXCURSION TRIP.

WICK TO KIRKWALL

BY THE FAVOURITE PASSENGER STEAMER,

"ST. CLAIR."

THE NORTH OF SCOTLAND & ORKNEY & SHETLAND STEAM NAVIGATION COMPANY, LTD.,

will run the above Steamer (unless prevented by any unforeseen occurrence) on

WEDNESDAY, 13TH JUNE, 1928,

AT 8 A.M., TO

SCAPA (KIRKWALL),

WHERE THE EXCURSIONISTS WILL BE LANDED.

The ST. CLAIR will LEAVE SCAPA on the RETURN TRIP at 5 p.m.

ARRIVING AT WICK ABOUT 8 P.M.

RETURN FARES - FIRST CABIN, **10**/-; SECOND CABIN, **6**/-

Intending Passengers are invited to procure their Tickets at the Company's Office, Wick, before the Holiday, or at least prior to going on board.

It is hoped that Friends from the Country will rally along for this Trip, got up as suitable for their leisure time for a Trip to a neighbouring County, at the minimum of cost.

Bicycles and Cars will be kept for the Excursionists in the Company's Stores, Wick.

ABERDEEN, 16th May, 1928.   JAS. McCALLUM, Manager.

J. HENDERSON, PRINTER, WICK.

St Clair (I) also offered occasional day excursion trips from Scrabster and from Wick to Scapa Pier.

In 1936, to free her name for her successor, *St Clair (I)* was renamed *St Colm*, and ran as such for a few months until sold for breaking up in Germany. She is seen here at Leith on 28 April 1937.

St Nicholas came in 1871 from J.G. Lawrie of Whiteinch, with machinery by Howdens, and was normally used as the summer west side steamer, and winter Caithness steamer.

St Nicholas aground at Wick. This card was posted in December 1903. On 17 June 1914 she ran aground again, and became a total loss when the tide went out.

In 1883 North Company took over the Pentland Firth service from the Highland Railway Co., who had taken the route over from George Robertson of Kirkwall in 1877. *St Olaf* was built in 1883 for this route by Murdoch & Murray of Port Glasgow with machinery by Dunsmuir and Jackson, but was reputedly underpowered, and only saw a relatively short spell of service on the route, being sold in 1890 to Quebec owners. She was lost at the mouth of the St Lawrence in 1900. (*G.E. Langmuir Collection, Mitchell Library*)

St Rognvald (I) was built in 1883, the first of many steamers built for the North Company by Hall Russell of Aberdeen. She was built for the weekend service, departing Leith and Aberdeen on a Friday for Kirkwall and Lerwick.

In 1886, *St Rognvald (I)* commenced a programme of Norwegian Fjord cruises for the North Company, and is seen here in that year at Bergen. *(Bård Kolltveit collection)*

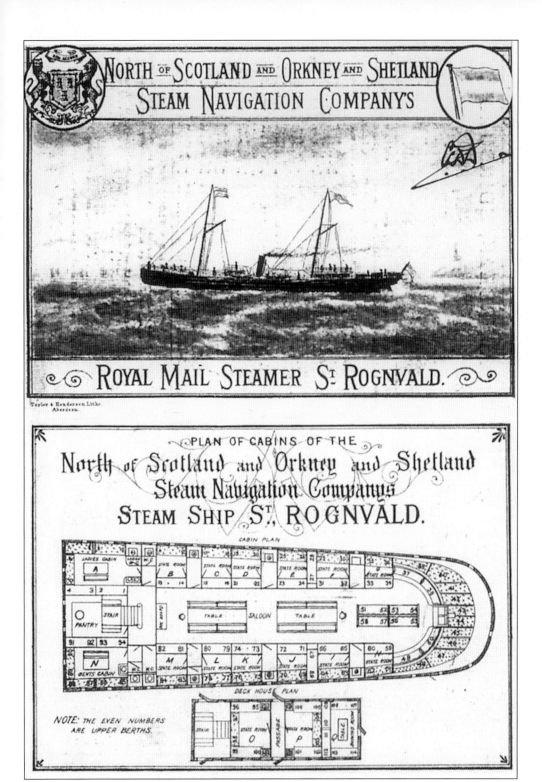

A copy of both sides of an advertising card featuring *St Rognvald (I)*, with a deck plan. (*G.E. Langmuir Collection, Mitchell Library*)

St Rognvald was wrecked on 24 April 1900 at Burgh Head, Stronsay.

The success of *St Rognvald*'s cruises led to the building in 1887 by Hall Russell of *St Sunniva (I)*, the first purpose-built cruise steamer in the world.

St Sunniva (I) at Odda in the Hardangerfjord, in the 1890s, with a steam launch in the foreground. (*Bård Kolltveit collection*)

St Sunniva (I) on one of her Norwegian cruises, seen at anchor off Gudvangen in the Sognefjord, August 1903.

In 1908 these cruises ceased, larger more luxurious competition by now having taken much of the traffic, and *St Sunniva (I)* was converted for the direct Lerwick service, with two hatches being built, and all-passenger accommodation removed from the lower deck. She is seen here, probably off Aberdeen, after this conversion.

Earl of Zetland (I) and *St Sunniva (I)* at Lerwick in a postcard view from the 1920s.

On 10 April 1930, St Sunniva (I) ran aground on the island of Mousa in fog en route north to Lerwick, and was unable to be salvaged.

ABERDEEN, EDINBURGH,
WICK, THURSO, ORKNEY, AND SHETLAND.

The NORTH OF SCOTLAND AND ORKNEY AND SHETLAND STEAM NAVIGATION COMPANY'S Powerful and Commodious Steamships are appointed to Sail in the following, or other order, during AUGUST, (unless prevented by any unforeseen occurrence), and calling, weather permitting, at the following Ports, but liberty is reserved to alter the arrangements as the necessities of the trade or any emergency may require.

Caithness, Orkney, and Shetland Passage.

From ALBERT DOCK, LEITH, and ABERDEEN, as under, carrying Her Majesty's Mails:—

		From Albert Dock, Leith.	From Aberdeen.
To Stromness and Scalloway,	ST. CLAIR,	1st Aug., at 12 noon	1st Aug., at 11 p.m.
To Wick, St. Margaret's Hope, and Thurso,	ST. NICHOLAS, 2nd „ at 1 p.m.		2nd „ at 12 night
To Kirkwall and Lerwick,	ST. MAGNUS, 3rd „ at 2 p.m.		3rd „ at 12 night
To Wick, Kirkwall, and Lerwick,	ST.ROGNVALD, 5th „ at 6 a.m.		5th „ at 4·30 p.m.
To Stromness and Scalloway,	ST. CLAIR, 8th „ at 6 a.m.		8th „ at 4·30 p.m.
To Wick, St. Margaret's Hope, and Thurso,	ST. NICHOLAS, 9th „ at 6 a.m.		9th „ at 4·30 p.m.
To Kirkwall and Lerwick,	ST. MAGNUS, 10th „ at 6 a.m.		10th „ at 5 p.m.
To Wick, Kirkwall, and Lerwick,	ST.ROGNVALD, 12th „ at 7·30 a.m.		12th „ at 7 p.m.
To Stromness and Scalloway,	ST. CLAIR, 15th „ at 11 a.m.		15th „ at 10 p.m.
To Wick, St. Margaret's Hope, and Thurso,	ST. NICHOLAS, 16th „ at 11 a.m.		16th „ at 11 p.m.
To Kirkwall and Lerwick,	ST. MAGNUS, 17th „ at 12 noon		17th „ at 12 night
To Wick, Kirkwall, and Lerwick,	ST.ROGNVALD, 19th „ at 2 p.m.		19th „ at 12 night
To Stromness and Scalloway,	ST. NICHOLAS, 22nd „ at 6 a.m.		22nd „ at 4·30 p.m.
To Wick, St. Margaret's Hope, and Thurso,	ST. CLAIR, 23rd „ at 6 a.m.		23rd „ at 4·30 p.m.
To Kirkwall and Lerwick,	ST. MAGNUS, 24th „ at 6 a.m.		24th „ at 4·30 p.m.
To Wick, Kirkwall, and Lerwick,	ST.ROGNVALD, 26th „ at 7·30 a.m.		26th „ at 7 p.m.
To Stromness and Scalloway,	ST. CLAIR, 29th „ at 11 a.m.		29th „ at 10 p.m.
To Wick, St. Margaret's Hope, and Thurso,	ST. NICHOLAS, 30th „ at 11 a.m.		30th „ at 11 p.m.
To Kirkwall and Lerwick,	ST. MAGNUS, 31st „ at 1 p.m.		31st „ at 12 night

RETURNING SOUTH AS FOLLOWS.

NOTE.—The Mondays' Sailings from Lerwick are via Kirkwall and Wick; the Saturdays' direct to Aberdeen; and the Wednesdays' or Thursdays' from Scalloway are via Stromness and Scapa Pier.

From LERWICK, every MONDAY and SATURDAY, viz.:—the 1st August, at 8 p.m.; the 6th at 10 p.m.; the 8th at 10 p.m.; the 13th at 6 p.m.; the 15th at 6 p.m.; the 20th at 10 p.m.; the 22nd at 10 p.m.; the 27th at 6 p.m.; the 29th at 6 p.m.; and 3rd September, at 10 p.m.

From HILLSWICK and VAILA SOUND (Walls), every WEDNESDAY.

From BRAE and VOE, WEDNESDAYS the 10th and 24th.

From SCALLOWAY, THURSDAYS the 4th, 11th, and 18th, at 6 a.m.; WEDNESDAYS the 24th and 31st, at 8 p.m.

From KIRKWALL, every TUESDAY, not before twelve hours after the posted time of leaving Lerwick.

From SCAPA PIER and STROMNESS, Evenings of THURSDAYS the 4th, 11th, and 18th; Mornings of THURSDAYS the 25th August and 1st September.

From THURSO, every THURSDAY at 6 a.m.

From ST. MARGARET'S HOPE every THURSDAY Forenoon

From WICK every TUESDAY Forenoon and THURSDAY Afternoon.

To ABERDEEN and ALBERT DOCK, LEITH.

Above and opposite page: A sailing list for August 1887, showing *St Clair* on the west side route to Stromness and Scalloway; *St Nicholas* on the Caithness route to Wick, St Margaret's Hope and Thurso; *St Magnus* on the Kirkwall and Lerwick service; and *St Rognvald* on the Wick, Kirkwall and Lerwick service. All sailings were from both Leith and Aberdeen. (*G.E. Langmuir Collection, Mitchell Library*)

SCRABSTER (THURSO), SCAPA, AND STROMNESS.

The Royal Mail Steamer, "St. Olaf," daily (Sunday excepted), leaves Stromness at 3·0 p.m., Scapa at 4·30 p.m., for Scrabster. Leaves Scrabster, not before 7·30 p.m., immediately after receiving Orkney Mails on board, and touches at South Ronaldshay.

Passage Fares—Scrabster to Scapa and Stromness,   1st Cabin 6/, 2nd Cabin 3/
           Scapa to St. Margaret's Hope & Stromness, ,,   2/   ,,   1/
           St. Margaret's Hope to Stromness, . ,,   3/   ,,   1/6
           St. Margaret's Hope to Scrabster, . ,,   4/   ,,   2/

From Aberdeen Harbour, to Albert Dock, Leith.

ST. MAGNUS,	Monday,	1st August,	at	1 a.m.
ST. ROGNVALD,	Wednesday,	3rd ,,	at	3 a.m.
ST. NICHOLAS,	Friday,	5th ,,	at	4 a.m.
ST. CLAIR,	Friday,	5th ,,	at	4 p.m.
ST. MAGNUS,	Monday,	8th ,,	at	1 a.m.
ST. ROGNVALD,	Wednesday,	10th ,,	at	6 a.m.
ST. NICHOLAS,	Friday,	12th ,,	at	8 a.m.
ST. CLAIR,	Friday,	12th ,,	at	3 p.m.
ST. MAGNUS,	Monday,	15th ,,	at	1 a.m.
ST. ROGNVALD,	Wednesday,	17th ,,	at	1 a.m.
ST. NICHOLAS,	Friday,	19th ,,	at	8 a.m.
ST. CLAIR,	Friday,	19th ,,	at	3 p.m.
ST. MAGNUS,	Monday,	22nd ,,	at	1 a.m.
ST. ROGNVALD,	Wednesday,	24th ,,	at	6 a.m.
ST. NICHOLAS,	Friday,	26th ,,	at	3 a.m.
ST. CLAIR	Friday,	26th ,,	at	8 a.m.
ST. MAGNUS,	Monday,	29th ,,	at	1 a.m.
ST. ROGNVALD,	Wednesday,	31st ,,	at	1 a.m.
ST. NICHOLAS,	Friday,	2nd September,	at	3 a.m.
ST. CLAIR,	Friday,	2nd ,,	at	3 p.m.
ST. MAGNUS,	Monday,	5th ,,	at	1 a.m.

Passage Fares—1st Cabin, 7s.; 2nd Cabin, 4s.

Passage Fares.—FROM ALBERT DOCK, LEITH.

	1st Cabin.	2nd Cabin.		1st Cabin.	2nd Cabin.
To Wick,	18/	9/	To Lerwick,	26/	10/6
To Thurso,	18/	9/	To Scalloway,	26/	10/6
To St. Margaret's Hope,	20/	9/	From Scalloway to places on West side,	5/	2/6
To Stromness,	20/	9/			
To Kirkwall,	20/	9/			

FROM ABERDEEN.

	1st Cabin.	2nd Cabin.		1st Cabin.	2nd Cabin.
To Wick,	12/	7/	To Kirkwall,	16/	7/
To Thurso,	12/	7/	To Lerwick,	21/	8/6
To St. Margaret's Hope,	16/	7/	To Scalloway,	21/	8/6
To Stromness,	16/	7/			
Between Intermediate Ports North of Scalloway or Lerwick,				2/	1/

Return Tickets available to return within three Calendar Months, are issued at the rate of a Single Fare and a half, except between Lerwick and the North Isles, with liberty to the holders to break the journey at any of the Ports of Call.

The Steamship "ORCADIA" sails twice a-week between KIRKWALL and the NORTH ISLES OF ORKNEY.
The Steamship "EARL OF ZETLAND" sails twice a-week between LERWICK and the NORTH OF SHETLAND.
First-class Hotel Accommodation at Wick, Thurso, Stromness, Kirkwall, Lerwick, and Scalloway; and the GRAND HOTEL at Lerwick is now open.

CHARLES MERRYLEES, Manager, Aberdeen.

North of Scotland & Orkney & Shetland Steam Navigation Co.'s Offices, Aberdeen, August, 1887.

In 1890 the North Company took over the Shetland Islands Steam Navigation Co., which operated *Earl of Zetland (I)* from Lerwick to the North Isles of Shetland. This steamer had been built by J. Fullerton of Paisley in 1877.

Lerwick pier with *Earl of Zetland (I)* to the left, *St Magnus (III)* astern of her, and a large crowd meeting the *St Sunniva (I)* arriving from Aberdeen.

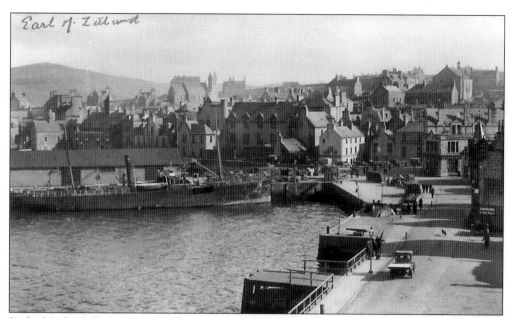

Earl of Zetland (I) at Lerwick. She served on the North Isles service until 1946, with annual winter diversions as relief steamer on the Pentland Firth service and, prior to 1914, occasional trips to Leith and Aberdeen. In 1939 she was renamed *Earl of Zetland II* to make way for her successor but, in fact, maintained her original service through the war years. In 1946 she was sold to a Panama company and renamed *Anal*, making one run of the blockade of Palestine with illegal Jewish immigrants. She was finally broken up in 1950.

The Argyll SS Co.'s *Argyll* was chartered in the 1891-1892 winter for the direct route from Aberdeen to Lerwick. She had been built in 1886 by Robert Duncan & Co. of Glasgow, and normally ran from Glasgow to Campbeltown and Stranraer. She was wrecked at Milleur Point at the entrance to Loch Ryan on 17 September 1893. *(Author's collection)*

St Ola (I) was built by Hall Russell in 1892 to replace *St Olaf* on the Pentland Firth service from Scrabster to Stromness, with calls at Scapa and, by ferry, at Hoxa, St Margaret's Hope.

St Ola (I) coming alongside Warehouse Pier, Stromness in 1910. (*G. Ellison collection, Orkney Natural History Society, Stromness*)

A postcard, posted in 1924, entitled 'Landing at Hoxa from *St Ola (I)* in Androo's Boat.' There was also a series of cartoons about this flit-boat. Hoxa was on South Ronaldsay and the flit-boat transferred passengers to St Margaret's Hope.

St Ola (I) departing Stromness for Scrabster. A postcard view, postmarked 1949, entitled 'Off in the morning, Stromness.' *St Ola (I)* was withdrawn in 1951 after a long and largely uneventful life on the route for which she was built, and was scrapped at Charlestown in that year.

St Giles (I) at Lerwick. She was also built in 1892 by Hall Russell for the direct Aberdeen to Lerwick service, and was lengthened around the turn of the century. On 28 September 1902, she ran aground near Rattray Head lighthouse in fog, broke her back, and was lost.

An unusual postcard view of the foredeck of *St Giles*, entitled 'Fisher Girls on the St Giles.'

St Ninian (I) came from Ramage & Ferguson of Leith in 1895 and was initially on the weekend service, but from 1897 to 1905, and again after 1920 she served as the secondary indirect boat in summer. Summers from 1906 to 1914 were spent on the west side run, and in summer from 1937 she was on the Caithness route. (From a North Company menu card)

St Ninian (I) remained in service until the Second World War. In both wars she was used as a naval transport between Scrabster and Scapa Flow. She was laid up after the war and was scrapped in 1948 at Rosyth.

1939

The North of Scotland & Orkney & Shetland Steam Navigation Co. Ltd.

☛ Passengers are carried subject to the conditions incorporated in the Company's Sailing Bills. ☚

WICK JUNE HOLIDAY

EXCURSION

FROM

WICK

TO

SCAPA

ON

MONDAY, 5th JUNE, 1939

AT 9 A.M.

By the S.S. "ST. NINIAN."

Returning from Scapa at 7 p.m.

RETURN FARES: 1st Cabin, 10/-
2nd Cabin, 6/-

Motor Bicycle & Side Car, 10/- Return.   Motor Bicycle, 6/- Return.

Ordinary Bicycle, 2/6 Return.

(Carried on Deck at Owner's Risk only)

Intending Passengers are invited to procure their tickets before sailing date, at the Company's Office, at Wick. These may also be secured before embarkation.

MATTHEWS' QUAY,
ABERDEEN.

JAMES L. SMITH,
Manager and Secretary.

By 1939, with *St Clair (I)* scrapped, *St Ninian (I)* was taking the annual Wick June Holiday day excursion from Wick to Scapa.

An 1898 advertisement for the North Company services and cruises. (*G.E. Langmuir Collection, Mitchell Library*)

TO TOURISTS.

STEAMERS TO

Caithness, Orkney, Shetland,

AND NORWAY

During Season 1898.

The "*St. Rognvald,*" "*St. Giles,*" "*St. Magnus,*" "*St. Nicholas,*" "*St. Ninian,*" "*St. Clair,*" "*St. Ola,*" and "*Queen,*"

SEVERAL TIMES A-WEEK TO

Wick, Thurso, Kirkwall, Stromness, Lerwick, and Scalloway.

The Mail Steamer, "ST. OLA," Daily between SCRABSTER PIER (Thurso), and SCAPA PIER and STROMNESS (Orkney).

The S.S. "EARL OF ZETLAND" Three times a-Week between LERWICK and the NORTH ISLES of SHETLAND.

FARES MODERATE.

All these Vessels have excellent accommodation for Passengers, and afford every facility for visiting the Islands of Orkney and Shetland.

NORWAY.

WEEKLY TOURIST SERVICE from LEITH and ABERDEEN, by the splendid new Steam-Ship "St. Sunniva," to the West Coast and Fiords of Norway.

For full particulars and Monthly Sailing Bills, apply to CHARLES MERRYLEES, *Manager, Aberdeen;* or to GEORGE HOURSTON, *Agent, 64, Constitution Street, Leith, and 18, Waterloo Place, Edinburgh.*

In 1900 the company had built the St Magnus Hotel at Hillswick, on the west coast of the Mainland of Shetland.

North of Scotland, Orkney, & Shetland Steam Navigation Company.

St. Magnus Hotel, Hillswick, Shetland.

S.S. St Nicholas

This is the Hotel We stay at as it is the only one too. it is all of wood both inside and out but Very nice and Comfortable a little too fashionable for Yours truly Break fast 9 Luncheon 1–30. Afternoon tea 4 Dinner 7–0

Opened 1900, under the Company's management, affords excellent accommodation for visitors at moderate rates. There is good and extensive loch and sea fishing in the neighbourhood. The coast scenery is grand. Tudor in his "Orkney and Shetland," published in 1883, page 533, says:— "When, as must come sooner or later, proper accommodation is provided throughout the length and breadth of Shetland for travellers in search of the beautiful, who will flock northwards, there will be no spot in all Hjaltland which in its manifold attractions will be so popular as 'Grey Hillswick.'" Apply to the Manageress of the Hotel, Hillswick.

An official North Company card showing *St Nicholas* and the St Magnus Hotel, Hillswick.

ARRIVAL   MANSON & CO., HILLSWICK

The arrival of the flit-boat from an unidentified North Company west side steamer at Hillswick with hotel guests.

Two
North Company Steamers
of the Twentieth Century

St Rognvald (II) was built in 1901 by Hall Russell to replace her wrecked predecessor of the same name. She is seen here in a postcard, posted in Kirkwall in 1908.

St Rognvald (II) in a gale, postmarked 1907. Another postcard view with a message stating 'This is what Kirkwall bay was like the day you arrived in Leith after your holiday.' She spent most of her career as the 'weekend boat', but also served the west side route in summers from 1925 to 1936.

'Farewell to Orkney.' A postcard view of a cow being loaded into the hold of *St Rognvald (II)*.

St Rognvald (II) from the cover of the 1929 North Company timetable.

From 1937 *St Rognvald (II)* had her funnel painted yellow, as in this postcard view at Stromness. During World War II she maintained a service from Aberdeen to Orkney and twice saw off attacks by German aircraft. In the summer of 1950 she ran from Leith and Aberdeen to Stromness and was withdrawn in October of that year, having been effectively replaced by *St Ninian (II)* and finally broken up at Ghent in 1951 after more than half a century of service.

St Giles (II) was built in 1903, again by Hall Russell, and replaced her predecessor of the same name, which had been wrecked the previous September, on the direct run year-round. She is seen here off Aberdeen.

In 1913 *St Giles (II)* was sold to the Government of Zanzibar, and was used as a yacht by the Sultan. She is seen here at what would appear to be Monte Carlo, still with the name *St Giles*. She was later renamed *Psyche*, and again *Khalifa*, before being scrapped in 1928.

St Magnus (II) was built in 1912 by Ramage & Ferguson of Leith and served on the secondary indirect route in summer. On 12 February 1918 she was sunk by enemy action off Peterhead whilst on passage from Lerwick to Aberdeen, with the loss of two passengers and one crew member. *St Margaret (I)* (not illustrated) came from the same builders a year later. During the First World War she was chartered to G. & J. Burns, and was torpedoed and sunk on 12 September 1917 whilst en route from Lerwick to Iceland. The surviving eighteen crew members made their way 150 miles back to Shetland in the ship's boat with an oar for a mast and part of the boat's cover for a sail.

In 1913 the cargo vessel *St Fergus* was built for the company by Hawthorn of Leith, but was sold to an Argentine company before completion. In 1916 she was re-purchased by the North Company, and served on the cargo services until sunk in a collision with *Fidra* off Rattray Head on 31 December 1940. (*G.E. Langmuir Collection, Mitchell Library, Glasgow*)

Another cargo steamer, *Cape Wrath*, not illustrated, was owned by the North Company from 1916 to 1927. She had been built at Ayr in 1900, and had various subsequent owners until she stranded in the River Severn in 1932 and was subsequently scrapped.

Express was a third wartime purchase. She had been built in 1869 at South Shields by Readhead Softley for George Robertson, who operated the Pentland Firth service prior to the Highland Railway Co. From 1877 to 1898 she operated from Kirkwall to various ports, and from 1899 to 1917 was chartered by WIlliam Cooper for a service from Kirkwall to Leith. She came into North Company ownership in early 1917, having earlier operated on charter to them for the Pentland Firth service from 1890 to 1892. She was lost off the French coast on 4 April of the same year. (*Alastair Cormack*)

In 1918 the North Company purchased a steamer named *Ape*. She had been built in 1898 by Barclay Curle for the Greenock to Belfast cargo service of G. & J. Burns. She became *Fetlar (I)* but was lost on 13 April 1919 on the Bunel Rocks near St Malo.

In the same year she was replaced by *Fetlar (II)*, which had been built in 1883 by Aitken & Mansel, with machinery by Muir & Caldwell, as *Cavalier* for the Glasgow to Inverness service of David MacBrayne Ltd. She did not last for long in the fleet as she was sold in March 1920 to the Dundalk & Newry Steam Packet Co. and was broken up in 1927. She is seen above as *Cavalier*.

44

In 1919 the North Company purchased MacBraynes' magnificent *Chieftain*. Ailsa of Troon had built her in 1907 for the Glasgow to Stornoway service. Renamed *St Margaret (II)*, she was not really a success with the company and operated the summer west side service for a few years, but was sold in 1925 to the Canadian National Steam Ship Co., and renamed *Prince Rupert*. In 1940 she went to the Union Steamship Co. of British Columbia, and became *Camosun*. She later went to Tel Aviv owners, and was finally broken up in 1952 after a final spell owned by a Panama flag company, which was reported to have operated her between Marseilles and Beira.

When she entered service in 1924, *St Magnus (III)* was the largest steamer in the fleet at 1,601gt. She was built by Hall Russell, and served as the summer weekend boat until 1939. She is seen here arriving at Lerwick with *St Sunniva (I)* on the left-hand berth.

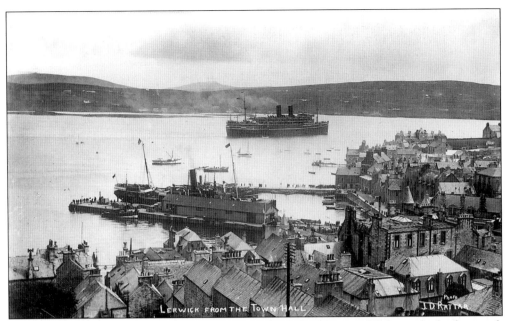

St Magnus (III) in a postcard view at Lerwick with P&O's *Viceroy of India* in the background.

An illustration of *St Magnus (III)* from a company menu card.

St Magnus (III), featured on a 1937 poster for excursions from Aberdeen to Leith during the Aberdeen Trades Holidays.

FROM MATTHEWS' QUAY, **ABERDEEN.**		
ST. NINIAN	Thursday, 15th JULY	4 p.m.
ST. CLAIR	Thursday, 15th ,,	10 p.m.
ST. CLAIR	Saturday, 17th ,,	11 a.m.
ST. ROGNVALD	Saturday, 17th ,,	11 a.m.
ST. NINIAN	Sunday, 18th ,,	12 noon
ST. SUNNIVA	Sunday, 18th ,,	12 noon
RETURNING FROM ALBERT DOCK, **LEITH.**		
ST. CLAIR	Sunday, 18th JULY	9 p.m.
ST. SUNNIVA	Monday, 19th ,,	10 a.m.
ST. NINIAN	Monday, 19th ,,	2 p.m.
ST. ROGNVALD	Tuesday, 20th ,,	2 p.m.
ST. MAGNUS	Thursday, 22nd ,,	3 p.m.
ST. NINIAN	Friday, 23rd ,,	12 noon
ST. CLAIR	Sunday, 25th ,,	4 p.m.

TICKETS ISSUED ALONGSIDE STEAMER 2 HOURS BEFORE ADVERTISED TIME OF SAILING

MEALS AND LIQUORS SUPPLIED ON BOARD AT REASONABLE PRICES

FULL PARTICULARS FROM

The North of Scotland & Orkney & Shetland Steam Navigation Co., Ltd.,

Phone 2860 Aberdeen   **Matthews' Quay, Aberdeen**

PASSENGERS ARE CARRIED SUBJECT TO THE CONDITIONS INCORPORATED IN THE COMPANY'S SAILING BILLS

The lower part of the above poster showing sailings from Aberdeen to Leith and back in July 1937.

S.S. ST. MAGNUS AT KIRKWALL.   3570

St Magnus (III) at Kirkwall. Around the late 1930s her funnel was painted yellow, like that of *St Rognvald (II)* and *St Sunniva (II)*. She was taken over by the Admiralty from 1939 to 1940 and took part in the Norwegian Campaign. During most of the war, she sailed from Aberdeen to Lerwick and was twice attacked by enemy aircraft. From 1945 she was on the main indirect run, and from 1950 on the weekend run again.

In the early 1950s *St Magnus (III)* was converted to oil firing, and was fitted with a shorter funnel. In 1960 she was sold for scrapping.

St Clement (I) was a cargo steamer built in 1928, and was similar to *St Fergus*. Unlike the latter, she could carry twelve passengers, and carried a mizzen mast. She was mainly identified with the winter Caithness service, and relieved *Earl Of Zetland* on the North Isles run each autumn for overhaul. She was sunk in an air attack on 3 April 1941, 20 miles south-east of Peterhead. Her chief engineer was lost. Note the grey hull in this photo. (*G.E. Langmuir*)

THURSDAY, JUNE 7, 1928

EVENING CRUISE

TO

VIEW ATLANTIC FLEET

R.M.S. "ST. OLA" (weather permitting) will leave the South Pier, at 7 p.m., and cruise round the Atlantic Fleet in Scapa Flow; returning about 10 p.m.

FARE, - 2s 6d.

Tickets will be issued at the Steamer's Office, on Thursday Evening, between the hours of 5 and 7 p.m.

JAMES McCALLUM,
Manager, ABERDEEN.

The presence of the Atlantic Fleet in Scapa Flow merited a special evening cruise from Scapa Pier by *St Ola* on 7 June 1928.

In 1930, following the loss of *St Sunniva (I)*, the North Company purchased *Lairdsbank* from Burns and Laird Line, and she became *St Catherine (I)*. She served initially on the west side run in the summer of 1930, but from then until sold for breaking up in 1937, she was laid up in summer and was on the direct run in winter. She had been built in 1893 on the Clyde by D. & W. Henderson as *Olive* for Laird Lines and originally operated from Glasgow to Londonderry, and later from Heysham to Londonderry. She is seen here approaching Scalloway, probably in the summer of 1930.

In 1931 a second *St Sunniva* was built by Hall Russell to replace her wrecked predecessor. With her white hull, clipper bow and figurehead, she looked every inch the luxury yacht. She is seen here arriving at Leith. From 1931 until 1937 she served on the summer direct service from Leith to Lerwick via Aberdeen.

St Sunniva (II) berthed at Leith Passenger Terminal.

The bow of *St Sunniva (II)*, showing the figurehead of the aforementioned saint. The outstretched arm could be removed when at sea, so as to avoid damage in heavy weather.

Next page: St Sunniva (II) off Aberdeen, probably in a builder's trials photo.

The dining saloon on *St Sunniva (II)*.

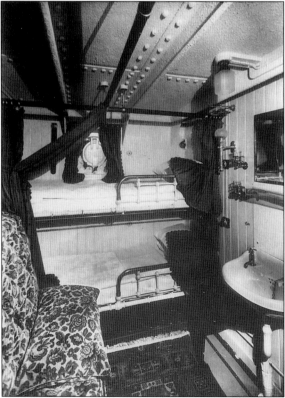

An outside cabin on *St Sunniva (II)*.

The cover of the North Company summer timetable for 1935, featuring *St Sunniva (II)*.

St Sunniva (II) featured in a company advertisement from an unknown source.

A pre-1937 view of Victoria Pier, Lerwick with *Earl of Zetland (I)*, *St Sunniva (II)* and *St Magnus (III)*.

St Sunniva (II) arriving at Lerwick, dressed overall, possibly on her maiden voyage. On the outbreak of war she was requisitioned by the Admiralty. She was used initially as an accommodation ship in Scapa Flow, and later as a convoy rescue ship, in which capacity she was lost with all hands on 22 January 1943. It is believed her masts and rigging iced over and she capsized because of the weight of the ice.

Built in 1937, *St Clair (II)* was the final steam-powered vessel to be built for the North Company, and is seen here departing Leith on her maiden voyage on 29 April of that year.

St Clair (II) arriving at Aberdeen in a storm, 10 February 1954. Prior to 1939 she had operated on the summer west side run, and the winter weekend run. During the war she became *HMS Baldur*, taking part in the occupation of Iceland, and later became a convoy rescue ship. After war service she was converted to oil-firing and served on the direct run from Aberdeen to Lerwick.

St Clair (II) at Lerwick Victoria Pier in a postcard view.

St Clair (II) in a 1950s postcard view at Lerwick. In 1960 she was briefly renamed *St Clair II*, and then *St Magnus (IV)*. In this postcard one can faintly make out the name *St Clair* on the bow, although the postcard caption says *St Magnus*.

St Magnus (IV) departing Aberdeen for Leith on 28 July 1966, at noon, her final day in service from Aberdeen for Leith.

An engine room of *St Magnus (IV)*, taken in 1966.

St Magnus (IV) retained her steam crane to the end, by which time it must have been one of the last such machines in existence.

In October 1966, *St Magnus (IV)* was renamed *St Magnus II*. (*Iain Quinn Collection*)

Although *St Clair* was the last steamship to be built for the North Company, a number of others were purchased second hand. *Highlander* had been built in 1916 by Caledon of Dundee for the Aberdeen, Newcastle & Hull Shipping Co., a subsidiary of the Dundee, Perth & London Co., in whose colours she is seen here at Aberdeen. In 1939 the North Company purchased her. She was attacked by German aircraft on 1 August 1940 and brought two of them down, sailing into Leith with the wreckage of one of them on her poop. She was renamed *St Catherine (II)*, and survived two more air attacks, but on 14 November 1940 she was sunk off Aberdeen. Her captain, thirteen members of her crew and one passenger were lost, while three passengers and fourteen of her crew were rescued.

Rora Head was also purchased in 1939. She had been built in 1921 by Day, Summers at Southampton for the General Steam Navigation Co., as *Blackrock*, and was sold to Comben Longstaff in 1937, and renamed *Brooktown*. She was almost immediately sold on to Leith owners who renamed her *Rora Head*. She survived the war and remained in the fleet until sold in 1956 when she was sold to Italian owners.

Amelia had been built in 1894 by S. McKnight of Ayr, with machinery by Muir & Houston. She had various owners in England and in Nova Scotia, Canada, and was wrecked in Canada in 1912. She was later salved and rebuilt, and in 1920 came under the ownership of W. Cooper & Son of Kirkwall, who maintained a cargo service from Leith to Aberdeen and Kirkwall. This company was taken over by the North Company in 1940 and *Amelia* continued on the route.

Amelia arriving at Leith in the early 1950s. She was withdrawn in 1955 after taking in water en route from Leith to Kirkwall. She had to put in to Aberdeen to avoid sinking and was broken up in the following year.

Dunleary had been built as a coastal collier in 1905 by A. & J. Inglis for Dublin owners. After sale shortly before the war to the Arran Steamship Co. of Irvine, the North Company purchased her in 1940. She was sold in 1947 to Greek owners, and sank off the coast of Cyrenacia in 1962.

Three
North Company Motorships

In 1939, the company's first motorship, *Earl of Zetland (II)* entered service, built by Hall Russell. She is seen here sailing out of Aberdeen on trials on 14 August 1939.

Earl of Zetland (II) at Lerwick on her first day in service, 14 August 1939. *Earl of Zetland (I)* is to the right and the funnel and masts of *St Magnus (III)* can be seen behind the pier. Within a couple of weeks she had been called up for war service on the Pentland Firth.

Earl of Zetland (II) maintained the North Isles service from Lerwick until the advent of the inter-island car ferries in the early seventies. She visited Aberdeen annually for overhaul, and is seen there on 31 January 1967.

Unst Boat Haven at Haroldswick is a museum of small boats. Amongst the exhibits here is a rowing boat, which served as the flit-boat conveying the passengers and cargo ashore from *Earl of Zetland (II)* at her calls at Baltasound or Uyeasound in Unst.

After withdrawal from service in 1973, *Earl of Zetland (II)* was sold for oil-related work and renamed *Celtic Surveyor*. She is seen here at Middlesbrough on 28 November 1976.

Celtic Surveyor then began a career as a floating pub, regaining the name *Earl of Zetland*. She spent some time in London's Docklands under the shadow of Canary Wharf and also at Eastbourne. She is now at North Shields Royal Quays, and is pictured there in October 2001.

St Clement (II) was the second motorship to join the North Company fleet and the first post-war newbuilding. She was built in 1946 by Hall Russell for cargo services, and also served as a relief steamer on the Pentland Firth and North Isles runs. She is seen here in a postcard view at Scrabster.

In the summers of the late sixties *St Clement (II)* served as an extra Pentland Firth ferry, and is seen here at Scrabster on 24 July 1968. She was sold to Greek owners in 1976, named *Gregoris*, and later *Melina*, and was broken up in 1984.

In 1950, *St Ninian (II)* was introduced. A product of the Caledon yard at Dundee, she served on the indirect run. She is seen here at in a postcard view at Kirkwall, with the steamer *Earl Thorfinn (1)* to the left.

St Ninian (II) at Leith, with a tall-funnelled Esso bunkering barge alongside.

St Ninian (II) canting as she departs Leith on 19 August 1966.

St Ninian (II) on the same occasion, now turned and ready to depart for Aberdeen, Kirkwall and Lerwick.

St Ninian (II) was sold in 1971 to Canadian owners Atlantique Cruise Lines Ltd of North Sydney, Nova Scotia, and operated on cruises to Saint Pierre and Miquelon, and to Newfoundland. She was not renamed and seemed little altered. After offering cruises in the summer seasons of 1971 and 1972, she was laid up.

The *M.V. St. Ninian* is the Fun Ship of the Eastern Coast. Informality is the keynote. On board the vessel features European first class accommodations for all cruise passengers (160) and it is not uncommon to rub elbows with the Captain or his officers, anytime during your cruise. A simple request can get you from the Bridge to the Engine Room, and if you are so inclined there is no objection if you feel like showing the piano player you can "Tickle The Ivories" too. The vessel features dancing and nightly entertainment, a games room where you may "try your luck"; three bars and lounges, a reading room, and most important to "My Lady" a bonded store for duty free shopping.

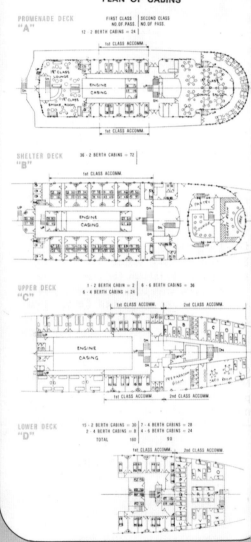

Detail from a Canadian cruise brochure for *St Ninian*,

MV ST. NINIAN

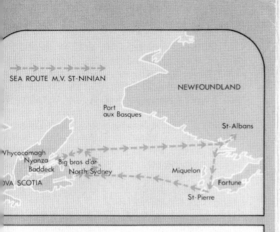

SEA ROUTE M.V. ST-NINIAN

NEWFOUNDLAND

Port aux Basques

St-Albans

Whycocomagh
Nyanza   Big bras d'or
Baddeck   North Sydney

Miquelon

OVA SCOTIA

Fortune

St-Pierre

DEPOSITS

25% deposit required at time of confirmation. Full payment 30 days prior to sailing.

CANCELLATIONS

All monies refunded if cancellation is received 15 days prior to sailing date. For complete refunds, purchase cancellation insurance as described.

Baggage Allowance : 150 lbs.
Embarkation Time : 1:30 pm
Pier : Public Wharf, North Sydney, N.S.

No pets allowed in cabins. Pets may be transported in the ship's kennels at set rates. Ask your Travel Agent for further details.

NOTE :

All passengers must register at the office of Atlantique Cruise Lines, Purves Street, North Sydney (adjacent to Public Wharf) to procure boarding passes and check baggage not later than 1:30 pm on the day of sailing.

GENERAL AGENTS :

CLARKE TRAFFIC SERVICES LTD.

1155 DORCHESTER W
MONTREAL, 102
876-5027

199 BAY ST.
TORONTO, ONT.
366-5673

SEE YOUR TRAVEL AGENT

CRUISES TO :

Saint Pierre et Miquelon

St. Albans, Newfoundland

Bras D'Or Lakes, Cape Breton

ATLANTIQUE CRUISE LINES LIMITED
P.O. Box 397   North Sydney, N.S.
(902) 794-7251

showing interior views and a deck plan.

In 1976, *St Ninian* was sold to Ecuador for cruising in the Galapagos Islands and was renamed *Bucanero* and also for a time, *Buccaneer*. She was latterly laid up for some years and was broken up at Guayaquil in 1991.

St Ola (II), the final ship in the post-war reconstruction scheme, entered service in May 1951, built by Alexander Hall & Co. of Aberdeen, and is seen here dressed overall on her maiden voyage.

St Ola (II) served the Scrabster to Stromness service for her entire career with the North Company, and is seen here at Scrabster.

In late winter and early spring, *St Ola (II)* would relieve *Earl of Zetland (II)* for overhaul, as in this illustration, where she is arriving at Lerwick from the North Isles on 2 February 1967.

In 1973 *St Ola (II)* became *St Ola II* to release the name for her successor. Two years later she was sold as an oil survey/research ship and was renamed *Aqua Star*, and is seen as such at Leith. In that role she sailed to the Mediterranean and to the east coast of Canada. She was scrapped at Vigo in 1987.

In 1955, *St Rognvald (III)* was introduced, again built by Alexander Hall & Co. of Aberdeen. Originally planned to be a fifty-passenger vessel, she emerged with a twelve-passenger capacity. She took over some of the duties of *St Clement (II)*, indirectly replacing the cargo steamers *Rora Head* and *Amelia*, and is seen here leaving Aberdeen on 1 August 1964 for Baltasound for a livestock sailing.

St Rognvald (III) leaving Kirkwall for Leith on 22 October 1965. At this time she was operating what was traditionally the secondary indirect service during the winter months.

Before the car ferries were introduced, cars had to be crane-loaded. A Mini van is here being loaded onto *St Rognvald (III)* at Aberdeen in 1966; note the row of new Minis in the background.

In 1978 *St Rognvald (III)* was sold to Gibraltar owners, renamed *Winston*, and converted to carry containers on a service from Shoreham to Gibraltar. She is seen here under that condition. In 1986 she was sold to Gambian owners and renamed *Washington*, and was again renamed *Radialo* in 1991 and became *Ras-Halague* later that year. Lloyds Register recorded her as being broken up in 2000.

The bow name of *Winston*, showing above it the name 'St Rognvald' painted over.

St Clair (III) was the final non-car-carrying vessel to be built for the North Company. She was built in 1960 by the Ailsa yard at Troon, and is seen here dressed overall for her maiden voyage. She served on the direct Aberdeen to Lerwick service.

In February 1970 *St Clair (III)*, relieved the Belfast Steamship Co.'s *Ulster Queen* and *Ulster Prince* for overhaul on the Liverpool to Belfast service. By this time Coast Lines Ltd owned both companies. She is seen here at Belfast, taken from Burns Laird's *Lion*, on 20 February 1970. (M.R. McRonald)

The following year, *St Clair (III)* again relieved on the Liverpool to Belfast service, and is seen here at Liverpool Landing Stage on 6 February 1971, with the Isle of Man Steam Packet's *Manx Maid*. (*M.R. McRonald*)

St Clair (III) was renamed *Al Khairat* when sold in 1977 and is seen here under that name at Grangemouth on 23 June 1977. She was converted to a livestock carrier, and was scrapped at Gadani Beach in Pakistan in 1987.

On 2 April 1977, *St Clair (III)* made her last sailing for what was now P&O Ferries from Lerwick to Aberdeen.

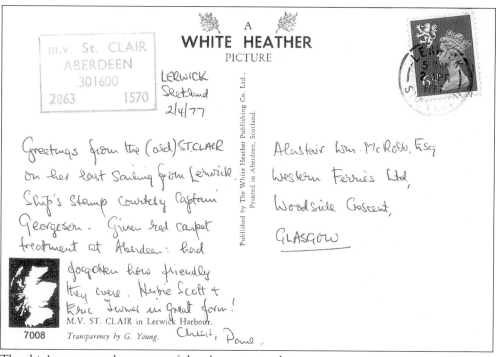

The ship's stamp on the reverse of the above postcard.

In 1966, *City of Dublin* was purchased from Palgrave Murphy of Dublin, and renamed *St Magnus (V)*, replacing the last steamer in the fleet, *St Magnus (IV)*. She had been built in 1955 and is seen here on her maiden voyage for the North Company, leaving Aberdeen for Leith on 4 April 1967.

St Magnus (V) arriving at Aberdeen from Kirkwall on 26 April 1967. She remained in the fleet until 1967 and was then sold for use in the Mediterranean and renamed *Mitera Eirini*. The same year she was again renamed *Dragon*, and she sank after a collision at the entrance to the Black Sea on 12 January 1979.

Four
The Car Ferry Era

The first car ferry in the North Company fleet was *St Ola (III)*, built in 1974 at Aberdeen for the Scrabster to Stromness crossing. She entered service on 29 January 1975, and is seen here the previous day on her first call at Scrabster on a special 'proving' run.

St Ola (II) arriving at Scrabster on 28 January 1975, her last day in service, with new *St Ola (III)* lying at the roro berth to the left.

In 1976, as the P&O Ferries identity took over, the funnel of *St Ola (III)* was painted light blue, as in this view at Scrabster.

By 1979, *St Ola (III)* had received a P&O Ferries logo on the superstructure.

After November 1980, the livery had altered to a light blue hull, and the P&O flag had appeared on the funnels.

St Ola (III) at Stromness in 1987.

St Ola (III) was fitted with side sponsons and a tank above the wheelhouse to increase her stability in February 1990. By this time the hull was dark blue and the initials P&O had replaced P&O Ferries as the logo. From 1989 the services had been marketed as P&O Scottish Ferries.

St Ola (III) was renamed *St Ola II* when withdrawn in early 1992, and later that year was renamed *Cecilia*. She saw a short period of service under charter on a service from Grenaa, Denmark to Helsingborg, Sweden. She is seen here laid up at Leith before this. She later became *Odigitria* for Ventouris Lines, and ran for one season for them in 1993, and was then sold to the Chinese Government.

Caledonian MacBrayne's *Clansman* relieved *St Ola* for overhaul in November each year from 1975 until 1982, and is seen here at Scrabster in October 1980.

The Roro freighter *Helga* was purchased in 1975 and renamed *Rof Beaver*. The name came from Roll on-roll Off, and Beaver was an old G. & J. Burns style animal name. She was the only vessel in the North Company fleet with this style of naming. She is seen here at Scrabster, deputising for *St Ola* after the latter had an engine room fire off Arran whilst returning from overhaul in November 1982. For that period passengers were carried by *Orcadia* and *St Magnus (VI)*.

Rof Beaver at Leith in June 1986. By 1990 she had been sold to Torbay Seaways and renamed *L Taurus*.

In 1973 a new car ferry for the Aberdeen to Lerwick service had been ordered from Hall Russell of Aberdeen, but the contract was later cancelled because of pressure of other work at the yard. In spring 1975 it was suggested that *Lion* from the Ardrossan to Belfast service be transferred here. The ferry which was eventually acquired by the company to be *St Clair (IV)* had been built in 1970 as *Peter Pan* for Travemünde-Trelleborg Line, as seen above, and had later operated as *SF Panther* for P&O Southern Ferries from Southampton to San Sebastian. When that service ceased in 1975, she was chartered to Da-No Line as *Terje Vigen* for service from Oslo to Aarhus in Denmark.

St Clair (IV) entered service on 4 April 1977, and is seen here at Lerwick in May of that year.

St Clair (IV) on 29 September 1979, by this time with P&O Ferries painted along her hull, at the lay by berth at the then new Holmsgarth roll on-roll off terminal to the north of Lerwick, with *Rof Beaver* to her right at the linkspan and the chartered livestock vessel *Angus Express* at the cattle berth to the far right.

St Clair (IV) in Aberdeen in August 1980, with the P&O flag being applied to the funnel.

In 1989 the hull of *St Clair (IV)* was painted dark blue with the P&O logo on it. She is here at Aberdeen in May 1990. She was withdrawn in early 1992 and sold to Malaysian owners, and renamed *Nusa Penjuang*, and was scrapped in 1999.

In 1978, the roro freight ferry *Dorset*, which had been built as *Donautal* in 1970, and had later sailed for the Belfast Steamship Co. as *Ulster Sportsman*, was chartered by the company, and was purchased when the charter period ended. She was named *St Magnus (VI)* and served on the indirect service, but with a call at Stromness rather than Kirkwall en route to Lerwick. She also served Hanstholm in Denmark and Kristiansand in Norway for a while. She is seen here at the west side of the North Pier in Stromness on 22 August 1979 from *St Ola (III)*.

St Magnus (VI) in 1981 with light blue hull at Holmsgarth, with *St Clair (IV)* behind her.

St Magnus (VI) leaving Scrabster in September 1988, with the flag now applied to the funnels. She regularly replaced *St Ola (III)* when the latter was in dock for annual overhaul. She was transferred to the Southampton to Le Havre route in June 1990, was sold to Danish owners later that year and immediately chartered to Polferries for the Swinoujscie to Ystad service. She was purchased by Polska Zeluga Baltycka in 1992 and renamed *Parseta*. In 1997 she was sold to Venezuelan ferry operator Conferrys and renamed *Dona Juana* for the service from the Venezuelan mainland to Margarita Island.

In 1987 a second passenger ferry was acquired for what was formerly known as the indirect route, and to give, along with *St Clair (IV)*, a daily service from Aberdeen to Lerwick, sailing twice weekly via Stromness. This was *St Sunniva (III)*. She had been built in 1971 as *Djursland* for Danish owners Jydsk Faergefart for a route from Grenaa to Hundested. In 1974 she became *Lasse II* for the same company's route from Kalundborg to Juelsminde. In 1979 she was sold to P&O and became *N F Panther* for the Dover to Boulogne route, and is seen here under that name.

In 1988 *St Sunniva (III)* made a special cruise to Glasgow for the Garden Festival, and is seen passing under the Erskine Bridge.

St Sunniva (III) on the Clyde at the Glasgow Garden Festival site with a tram in the background, where she remained strikebound for some time.

St Sunniva (III) at Stromness in May 1999. Her weekend indirect sailings were marketed as two islands mini-cruises, leaving Aberdeen at 12.00p.m on a Saturday, arriving at Stromness in the late evening, leaving Stromness for Lerwick at 12.00p.m on the Sunday, allowing time for a coach tour of Orkney in the morning. The return from Lerwick to Aberdeen was made at the scheduled time of 6.00p.m. on a Monday.

A quayside view of *St Sunniva (III)* at Stromness on the same occasion.

A deck view on *St Sunniva (III)* en route from Stromness to Lerwick in May 1999.

In 1990 the freight ferry *Marino Torre* was chartered by P&O Scottish Ferries. She had been built in 1970 as *Rhonetal*, and had operated as *Norcape* (for North Sea Ferries), *Rhonetal*, and *Rhone* prior to becoming *Marino Torre* in 1987.

In 1990 *Marino Torre* was purchased by the company and renamed *St Rognvald (IV)*, in this view at Aberdeen in that year. She is berthed at the Eurolink ramp, the second linkspan at the port.

St Rognvald (IV) eventually replaced *St Magnus (VI)* in the fleet, offering a single round trip per week and occasionally filling her time mid-week with charters, e.g. to Ferrymasters for a Middlesbrough to Gothenburg service in 1993 and to Fjord Line as a back-up freight ferry from North Shields to Bergen in 1994. At weekends she spent time at Lerwick, as here in May 1999.

In 1992 the two main members of the fleet were replaced. *St Ola (III)* was replaced by *Eckerö* of Eckerö Lines of Finland, running from Grisslehamn in Sweden to Eckerö on the Åland Islands. She had been built in 1971 as *Svea Scarlett* for the Copenhagen to Landskrona route.

She was renamed *St Ola (IV)* and took over the Scrabster (above) to Stromness route of her predecessor on 25 March 1992.

St Ola (IV) at Scrabster with the excursion ship *Balmoral*, which had stopped to offer an evening cruise during a positioning voyage round the British coast, in July 1993. *(Ian Somerville)*

St Ola (IV) and *St Sunniva (III)* at Stromness on a wet Sunday morning in May 1999.

St Clair (V) had also been built in 1971, as *Travemünde* for Gedser-Travemünde Ruten. Ten years later she was sold to Yugoslavian owners and renamed *Njegos*, and in 1984 was chartered to Sally Line for the Ramsgate to Dunkirk service. In 1985 she was chartered to Brittany Ferries as *Tregastel*, in which guise she is seen here, departing from Roscoff. In 1987 the latter firm purchased her.

St Clair (V) replaced her predecessor of the name on the Aberdeen to Lerwick service in March 1992. She is seen here at Aberdeen along with the Faeroese ferry *Smyril*. (*Ian Somerville*)

In the summer peak season from 1993 to 1997 *St Clair* (V) operated a weekly extension to her service from Lerwick to Bergen. A view at Aberdeen in May 2001.

Five
Chartered Vessels
and Competitors

The paddle steamer *Ben My Chree (I)*, in May 1860, of the Isle of Man Steam Packet Co., which had been sold earlier that year to shipbuilders Tod & McGregor. It was advertised to sail every Friday from Granton to Aberdeen, Cullen, Lossiemouth, Burghead, Nairn, Cromarty, Invergordon, Chanory Point (Fort George) and Inverness. There was no indication in the advert of who was actually operating her, but her agents at Granton were the North Company, and at Aberdeen the Aberdeen Steam Navigation Co. Robert Napier of Glasgow had built her in 1845. Following her spell of service to the Moray Firth, *Ben My Chree* was operational in West Africa, and later converted to a hulk. Her remains were still reported to be visible at Bonny in Nigeria as late as 1930. She was one of a number of steamers operating to Moray Firth ports in that era, details of which have still to be researched. The North Company had operated to Inverness up to 1859, the railway link to that town having been opened in the previous year.

A postcard entitled 'A visitor to Stromness'. A.W. McRobb notes that this is 'almost certainly *Duke of Connaught (1)* (1902) which called at Stromness on a cruise from Heysham to Aberdeen and Hull (?) on 13 June 1932.' She had been built for the L&YR/LNWR joint service from Fleetwood to Belfast.

The Faeroe Steamship Co.'s steamer *Tjaldur* operated on the Pentland Firth service from June 1943 until 1946. At this time the crossing was operated as a four-ship service. She had been built in 1916 as *St Thomas* for Danish owners and in 1920 became *Baltannic* of the United Baltic Co., and was sold to the Faeroe Steamship Co. shortly before the war.

Also making an appearance on the Pentland Firth during the war years was the Norwegian steamer *Galtesund*, seen here at Oslo in 1938. She had escaped German-controlled Norway by being seized by Norwegian resistance fighters whilst en route from Oslo to Bergen on 15 March 1942. They took the vessel to Shetland. She had been built in 1906 by Burmeister & Wain at Copenhagen as *Skandia* for Danish owners. She later became *Skandia II*, and was sold to Arendal Dampskipsselskap in 1918 and renamed *Galtesund*. She returned to Norway in 1945 and sailed for another ten years. (*Bård Kolltveit collection*)

On 16 December 1944 two further steamers were allocated to the North Company as military transports. One of these was *Nova* of the Bergen Steamship Co., which operated from Aberdeen to the Faeroes until September 1945. She had been built in 1925 and operated from Norway to Iceland. After being returned to her owners, she was converted to oil-firing in January 1948 and was wrecked on the Norwegian coast on 19 December 1949 en route from Antwerp to Stavanger.

The final steamer to commence operating for the North Company during the war was *Lochnagar* of the Aberdeen Steam Navigation Co. Ltd. She was the second steamer to be allocated to the company on 16 December 1944, and operated from Aberdeen to Lerwick until February 1946. John Browns at Clydebank had built her in 1906 for G. & J. Burns as *Woodcock* for the Ardrossan to Belfast service. In 1928, after the formation of Burns & Laird Lines, she was renamed *Lairdswood*, and in 1930 sold to the Aberdeen Steam Navigation Co. and entered service as *Lochnagar* the following June. She was sold in 1946 to Egyptian Panama-flag owners as *Rena* and made one trip in 1948 with emigrants from Piraeus to Buenos Aires and one from Genoa to Melbourne, returning via Hong Kong and Shanghai. She was renamed *Blue Star* in 1952, and was broken up in the same year.

The livestock carrier *Shorthorn Express* (1957) was one of a number of livestock carriers chartered for autumn cattle sailings from 1977 onwards, and is seen here leaving Aberdeen.

Another chartered livestock carrier was *Frisian Express* (1957), seen on the Clyde passing under a partially completed Erskine Bridge in 1969.

Irish Provider (1964), yet another livestock ship, seen in 1993 with the stern of *St Rognvald* in the background.

Following the demise of *Earl of Zetland (II)*, the full series of car ferry crossings operated by Zetland Island Council had not yet commenced, as terminals were not yet ready at Symbister (Whalsay) and Laxo (Mainland). The car ferry *Grima* was chartered to the North Company to operate a Lerwick to Symbister service from February 1975 until January of the following year. She is seen here at Bressay. *(Ian Somerville)*

The Faeroese ferry *Smyril*, seen here at Aberdeen, has been chartered on occasion to cover vessels away on overhaul. *(Ian Somerville)*

Smyril with *St Ola (III)* at Scrabster. She was built in 1969 as *Morten Mols*, one of a quartet for Danish operator Mols Line.

Smyril in Aberdeen in spring 1992, with the then newly acquired P&O ships *St Clair (V)* and *St Ola (IV)*. She also operated a service from Torshavn to Scrabster from 1976 until replaced on international routes by Smyril Line's *Norröna* in 1983.

In December 1985, a service was started from Kirkwall to Scalloway with *Syllingar*, which was built in 1956 as *Scillonian* for the Isles of Scilly Steamship Co., and had been sold in 1977 to P&A Campbell for excursion work on the Bristol Channel as *Devonia*, and then again in 1981 to Torbay Seaways as *Devoniun* to operate from Torquay to Guernsey. The operator from Orkney to Shetland was Norse Atlantic Ferries, and the service only lasted until May 1986, after which time she was laid up in the East India Harbour at Greenock as seen here. She was later sold to Greek operators and renamed *Remvi*.

A short sea passenger ferry service was started across the Pentland Firth from John O'Groats to Burwick in the early 1970s with the small motor boat *Pentalina*.

In 1976, *Pentalina* was replaced by *Souters Lass*, which had been built in 1948 as *Bournemouth Belle* for service at Bournemouth, and was later *Weymouth Belle* at Weymouth from 1967 to 1974.

In 1987, the newly built *Pentland Venture* replaced *Souters Lass*, which was later sold to operate seal-watching trips out of Fort William. The former vessel was later lengthened. These sailings by John O'Groats Ferries, operate in connection with a bus connection northwards from Inverness, and on to Kirkwall from Burwick, road improvements in the past two decades giving the possibility of day excursions from Inverness to Kirkwall and vice versa.

In 1989 a car ferry service was started by Orkney Ferries, a company backed by Orkney Islands Council, across the Pentland Firth short sea crossing, using the newly-built *Varagen* from Houton to Gills Bay, west of John O'Groats. The service lasted only a couple of weeks before the exposed linkspan at Gills Bay was damaged during a storm. *Varagen* is seen here in Orkney Ferries colours.

In 1998 Caledonian MacBrayne's *Iona* was purchased by a new company named Pentland Ferries, and renamed *Pentalina B*, but they did not begin operation until May 2001 on a route from St Margaret's Hope to a new more protected terminal at Gills Bay. She is seen here at St Margaret's Hope in summer 2001.

Six
Orkney Inter-Island Ferries

S.S. Orcadia, Orkney.

Steamer services to the North Isles of Orkney were commenced in 1865 by George Robertson with *Orcadia (I)*. In 1868 the steamer and service was taken over by the Orkney Steam Navigation Co., who had *Orcadia (II)* built in the same year by Readhead Softley on the Tyne. She is seen here after lengthening by 20ft and re-engining by Hall Russell in 1884.

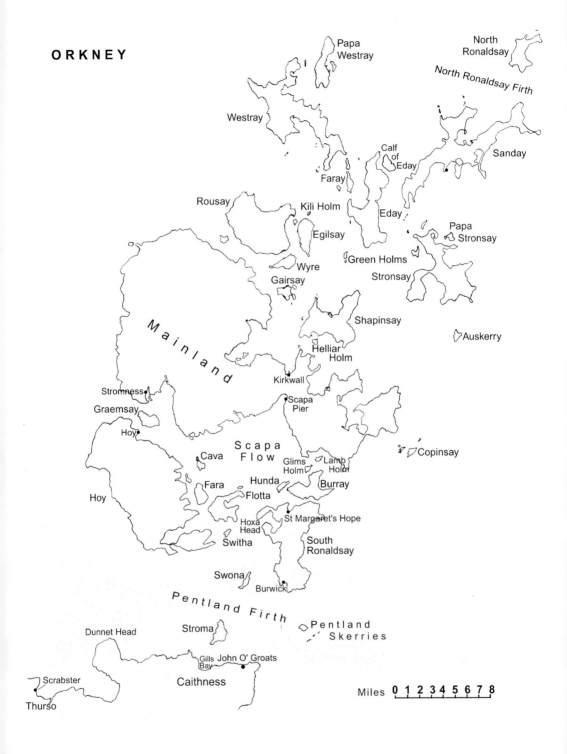

ORKNEY

Papa
Westray

North
Ronaldsay

North Ronaldsay Firth

Westray

Calf
of
Eday

Sanday

Faray

Rousay

Kili Holm

Eday

Papa
Stronsay

Egilsay

Green Holms

Wyre

Stronsay

Gairsay

M a i n l a n d

Shapinsay

Auskerry

Helliar
Holm

Kirkwall

Stromness

Scapa
Pier

Graemsay

Hoy

Copinsay

S c a p a
F l o w

Cava

Glims
Holm

Lamb
Holm

Fara

Hunda

Burray

Hoy

Flotta

Hoxa
Head

St Margaret's Hope

Switha

South
Ronaldsay

Swona

Burwick

P e n t l a n d   F i r t h

Dunnet Head

Stroma

P e n t l a n d
S k e r r i e s

Gills
Bay

John O' Groats

Scrabster

Caithness

Thurso

Miles 0 1 2 3 4 5 6 7 8

A map of Orkney. (*Alastair Cormack Collection – originally published in* Days of Orkney Steam, *1971*)

110

Orcadia (II) was easily recognisable by her whale-back fo'c'sle. She maintained services to the northern isles of Westray, Sanday, Stronsay, and Eday until 1931, when she was sold to Kirkwall owners. After a couple of months on charter replacing *Cormorant* on the Western Isles supply boat service of Robert Garden, she was used as a coal hulk at Stronsay until scrapped at Bo'ness in 1934. (*Alastair Cormack Collection*)

In 1892, *Fawn* was purchased by the Orkney Steam Navigation Co. to serve Rousay. She had been built in Germany in 1869, and remained in service until 1917, when she was sold. She was replaced in 1919 by *Countess of Bantry* (not illustrated), which had been built in 1884 by Workman Clark of Belfast for a service from Bantry to Castletownbere, and was later on excursion work at Oban. She served the North isles until 1928 and was scrapped in 1934. (*G.E. Langmuir*)

In 1928, *Orcadia (II)* finally got a replacement, *Earl Thorfinn (I)*, built at Aberdeen by Hall Russell. She remained in service until 1963, and was then broken up at Bo'ness on the Forth.

1930 saw a second steam Earl appear, *Earl Sigurd (I)*. She enabled *Orcadia (II)*, which had been used as a reserve steamer for the previous two years, to be withdrawn and by the time of her withdrawal in 1969 she was probably the last coal-fired commercially operated steamer in existence in British waters. (*Alastair Cormack Collection*)

ORKNEY STEAM NAVIGATION COMPANY, LTD.

Sailings for September, 1947

NOTE.—The Round of the Islands is made on Fridays   Mails and Passengers only conveyed on those days. Fare for the Round Trip, 12/3.

The Steamers "Earl Thorfinn" and "Earl Sigurd" or other conveyance will (unless prevented by any unforeseen occurrence) sail as follows:

MONDAY, September 1

| From Westray | 6.30 a.m. | From Sanday | 9.30 a.m. |
| " Papa Westray | 7 a.m. | " Stronsay | 10.45 a.m. |

and Eday Pier **noon**, for Kirkwall

WEDNESDAY, September 3

From Kirkwall .... at 6.45 a.m.
For Stronsay, Sanday, Eday Pier, Papa Westray and Westray.

THURSDAY, September 4

| From Westray | 7 a.m. | From Calfsound | 8.15 a.m. |
| " Papa Westray | 7.30 a.m. | " Stronsay | 9.30 a.m. |

and Sanday 10.45 a.m., for Kirkwall.

FRIDAY, September 5

From Kirkwall .... at 6.15 a.m.

| From Westray | 9.15 a.m. | From Sanday | 11.45 a.m. |
| " Papa Westray | 9.45 a.m. | " Stronsay | 12.45 p.m. |

and Eday Pier 2 p.m., for Kirkwall.

SATURDAY, September 6

From Kirkwall .... at 6.45 a.m.
For Stronsay, Sanday, Calfsound, Papa Westray Pier & Westray.

MONDAY, September 8

| From Westray | 6.30 a.m. | From Sanday | 9.15 a.m. |
| " Papa Westray | 7 a.m. | " Stronsay | 10.30 a.m. |

and Eday Pier **noon**, for Kirkwall

WEDNESDAY, September 10

From Kirkwall .... at 6.45 a.m.
For Eday Pier, Sanday, Stronsay, Papa Westray and Westray.

THURSDAY, September 11

| From Westray | 6.30 a.m. | From Calfsound | 8.15 a.m. |
| " P. West'y Pier | 7.30 a.m. | " Sanday | 9.30 a.m. |

and Stronsay 10.45 a.m., for Kirkwall

FRIDAY, September 12

From Kirkwall .... at 6.45 a.m.

| From Eday Pier | 8.45 a.m. | From Sanday | 10.45 a.m. |
| " Stronsay | 9.45 a.m. | " Papa Westray | 12.45 p.m. |

and Westray 1.15 p.m. for Kirkwall

SATURDAY, September 13

From Kirkwall .... at 6.45 a.m.
For Sanday, Stronsay, Calfsound, Papa Westray and Westray

MONDAY, September 15

| From Westray | 7 a.m. | From Sanday | 10 a.m. |
| " Papa Westray | 7.30 a.m. | " Stronsay | 11.15 a.m. |

and Eday Pier 12.30 p.m., for Kirkwall.

WEDNESDAY, September 17

From Kirkwall .... at 6.45 a.m.
For Stronsay, Sanday, Eday Pier, Papa Westray and Westray.

THURSDAY, September 18

| From Westray | 7 a.m. | From Calfsound | 8.15 a.m. |
| " Papa Westray | 7.30 a.m. | " Stronsay | 9.30 a.m. |

and Sanday 10.45 a.m., for Kirkwall.

FRIDAY, September 19

From Kirkwall .... at 6.15 a.m.

| From Westray | 9.15 a.m. | From Sanday | 11.45 a.m. |
| " Papa Westray | 9.45 a.m. | " Stronsay | 12.45 p.m. |

and Eday Pier 2 p.m. for Kirkwall.

SATURDAY, September 20

From Kirkwall .... at 6.45 a.m.
For Stronsay, Sanday, Calfsound, Papa Westray Pier & Westray

MONDAY, September 22

| From Westray | 6.30 a.m. | From Sanday | 9.15 a.m. |
| " Papa Westray | 7 a.m. | " Stronsay | 10.30 a.m. |

and Eday Pier **noon**, for Kirkwall

WEDNESDAY, September 24

From Kirkwall .... at 6.45 a.m.
For Eday Pier, Sanday, Stronsay, Papa Westray and Westray.

THURSDAY, September 25

| From Westray | 6.30 a.m. | From Calfsound | 8.15 a.m. |
| " P. Wert'y Pier | 7.30 a.m. | " Sanday | 9.45 a.m. |

and Stronsay 11 a.m., for Kirkwall

FRIDAY, September 26

From Kirkwall .... at 6.45 a.m.

| From Eday Pier | 8.45 a.m. | From Sanday | 10.45 a.m. |
| " Stronsay | 9.45 a.m. | " Papa Westray | 12.45 p.m. |

and Westray 1.15 p.m. for Kirkwall.

SATURDAY, September 27

From Kirkwall .... at 6.45 a.m.
For Stronsay, Sanday, Calfsound, Papa Westray and Westray.

MONDAY, September 29

| From Westray | 7 a.m. | From Eday Pier | 9.15 a.m. |
| " Papa Westray | 7.30 a.m. | " Sanday | 10.45 a.m. |

and Stronsay **noon**, for Kirkwall

KIRKWALL AND ROUSAY

		From Rousay.	From Egilshay.
WEDNESDAY,	3rd Sept.	noon	12.30 p.m.
WEDNESDAY,	10th Sept.	8 a.m.	8.30 a.m.
MONDAY,	15th Sept.	9.30 a.m.	7.30 a.m.
MONDAY,	22nd Sept.	7 a.m.	7.30 a.m.
MONDAY	29th Sept.	9.30 a.m.	7.30 a.m.

NOTICE IS HEREBY GIVEN, that the Company will not be responsible for any accident, loss or damage sustained by persons coming on board or disembarking from their boats, or shipping animals or goods by boat, at any other place than the ports of call specified in the foregoing notice, and persons boarding the Company's Steamers, except at the regular ports of call, do so at their own risk.

Passengers and their luggage are only carried on the terms of the conditions printed on the back of the passenger tickets.

The Company reserve the right to deviate from the advertised routes as the exigencies of the trade or weather conditions may require.

As the steamers will leave Kirkwall at the hour advertised, Shippers are requested to have their goods alongside half-an-hour before sailing time.

D. BERTRAM, *Manager.*

Printed at *The Orcadian* Office, Victoria Street, Kirkwall

A list of sailings for September 1947 by *Earl Thorfinn* (I) and *Earl Sigurd* (I). (G.E. Langmuir collection, Mitchell Library, Glasgow)

On 1 January 1962, the Orkney Islands Shipping Co. took over from the Orkney Steam Navigation Co., and later that year new, diesel-powered *Orcadia (III)* took over from the by now anachronistic steamer *Earl Thorfinn (I)*. *Orcadia (III)* was actually owned by the Secretary of State for Scotland.

Orcadia (III) was chartered to P&O in November 1982 after *St Ola (III)* had the aforementioned engine room fire off Arran. She is seen here at Wick on 19 November 1982 having arrived from Kirkwall. *Orcadia(III)* was withdrawn in 1990, was laid up at Leith for a while, and was then sold to owners in the Caribbean in 1994.

In 1969, a twelve-passenger cargo ship replaced *Earl Sigurd (I)*. *Islander* was built by J. Lewis & Co. at Aberdeen, and remained in service until 1991. She served North Ronaldsay, Egilsay and Wyre, and as relief vessel for *Orcadia*. She was laid up until 1993 when she was sold to Honduras-flag owners for whom she continues to sail as *Mary Pal*. *(Alastair Cormack Collection)*

A composite postcard issued by the Orkney Islands Shipping Co. Ltd in the 1970s. Top left: *Orcadia (III)*. Top right: *Lyrawa Bay*. She had been built as the Faeroese vessel *Sam*. She was purchased in 1976, and converted to a small stern-loading car ferry for the route from Houton to Lyness on Hoy. Withdrawn in 1991, she was sold to a fish farm owner. Lower left: *Islander*. Lower right: *Clytus*.

By 1990, *Orcadia (III)* was getting dated, and there was a demand for a roll-on roll-off service to the North Isles. A pair of new Earls were built for these services. *Earl Sigurd (II)* is seen at Kirkwall.

Earl Thorfinn at Rapness pier on Westray. *(Ian Somerville)*

The following year *Varagen* joined the two Earls after the failure of the Orkney Ferries service from Houton to Gills Bay. The entry into service of this third roro vessel enabled *Islander* to be sold. *(Craig Taylor, Alastair Cormack Collection)*

Iona was the Kirkwall to Shapinsay mail steamer for many years. She was built locally in 1893 by T.B. Stevenson for John Reid, and was taken over in 1914 by William Dennison. In 1949 she was dieselised, and lasted until November 1964 when she sank in a storm at Shapinsay pier at the age of seventy-one.

Klydon was built in 1963 at Cologne in Germany for Dennison's Kirkwall to Shapinsay service. She was floated down the Rhine to Dordrecht where her Danish-made machinery was fitted. She was the fourth vessel of that name on the route, there previously having been a sailing smack and two motor boats. In April 1969, whilst on charter to Alginate Industries, she ran aground at Tarbert, Harris, whilst manoeuvring to avoid MacBrayne's *Hebrides*, which was berthing. She was salvaged and taken to Stornoway, and sold to her charterers. They renamed her *Alga*. She remains in Lloyds Register under that name, owned by A.R. Robinson of Stornoway.

The Shapinsay route was taken over by the Orkney Islands Shipping Co. in 1970, and *Clytus* was acquired for it. She had been built in 1944 as the Clyde pilot cutter *Gantock*. She was purchased by the Secretary of State for Scotland and converted to a passenger launch. She served there until withdrawn in 1987, when she was sold to a diving company.

Shapinsay was built in 1989 at Hull for the Shapinsay service. She is seen here arriving at Kirkwall in her original colours with the displaced *Clytus* to the left. *(Ian Somerville)*

Eynhallow inaugurated roll on roll off services from Tingwall to Rousay, Egilsay and Wyre in 1987. In 1991 she was lengthened by 5m. She is seen here at Rousay on 31 August 1994.

Saga was built in 1893 for the South Isles Steam Packet Co. for the Stromness to Longhope service. She was not particularly reliable and only lasted on the route until August 1895 when she was sold to the Cromarty Steamship Co. for the Cromarty to Invergordon service. She was purchased by the Admiralty in the First World War, and shipped out to the Dardanelles, and spent time after that conflict in the Mediterranean. In the early 1920s she came back to the Clyde and served as a scrap boat. She was scrapped herself in 1939, and is seen here at Port Bannatyne on Bute. (*G.E. Langmuir collection, Mitchell Library, Glasgow*)

Hoy Head (I) was built in 1896 by Seath of Rutherglen for Robert Garden, who started a new service to the South Isles with her in that year. She sailed from Stromness to Graemsay, Longhope and Flotta four days a week, with, from the First World War onwards, a weekly call at St Margaret's Hope and Scapa. In 1919 she, and the route she served, was sold to the Stromness & South Isles Steam Packet Co., in 1921 to Swanson & Towers, and in 1938 to Bremner & Co. Not until 1956 was she scrapped at Granton. (*Alastair Cormack Collection*)

Bremners saw a major expansion of traffic during the Second World War and after. Two steam drifters, *Pride O' Fife* and *Premier* were purchased in 1940 and, in 1943, the coaster *Wisbech*. In 1947 the South Isles got their own *Orcadia*. Bremner's *Orcadia* had been built in 1905 as the Admiralty tender *Playfair*, used to serve Inchkeith in the Firth of Forth. This enabled *Hoy Head* to be placed in reserve. She was sold in 1958 to a Buckie firm of shipbuilders who intended to re-engine her and convert her to a fishing boat, but that proved impracticable, and she was sold for scrapping at Peterhead. (*Alastair Cormack Collection*)

Also purchased in 1947 was the cargo steamer *Cushag*. She had been built in 1908 by George Brown & Co. of Greenock as *Ardnagrena* for Belfast owners. In 1920, after two intermediate changes of ownership, she was purchased by The Isle of Man Steam Packet Co. Ltd, in whose colours she is seen here, at the cargo berth at Douglas. In 1943 she was sold again to Stornoway owners. She lasted seven years with Bremners, was sold in 1954 to Dundee owners, and broken up at Granton in 1957. Her Orkney service, and that of the other coasters of Bremners, included the taking south of sections of wooden huts dismantled after war service, and of scrap, and carrying cargoes of coal from north-east England ports to Orkney. (*John Shepherd Collection*)

Four further steam coasters joined Bremner's fleet in the 1950s. *Orkney Trader* was purchased in 1952. She had been built in 1908 in Dublin for Dundalk owners as *Carlingford*, sold to Liverpool owners in 1934, and again to Belfast owners in 1946 for whom she sailed as *Third*. She was sold and broken up at Dublin in 1959.

Orkney Dawn (I) was purchased in 1953. She had been built in 1921 by Cook, Welton & Gemmell at Beverley for Liverpool owners as *Redesmere*, sold to Bristol owners in 1926 as *Brockley Combe*, and again in 1937 to George Couper of Helmsdale for whom she ran as *Lothdale*. In 1947 she was sold again to Aberdeen owners without change of name. She was sold in 1955 to Whitehaven owners and renamed *Cumbria*, and was scrapped in 1957 at Troon.

Orkney Dawn (II) was purchased in 1955. She had been built in 1916 by Cochrane of Selby for Hull owners as *Magrix*, and sold to Aberdeen owners in 1937 as *Deedon*, and again to other Aberdeen owners in 1946. She was sold in 1957 for scrapping at Passage West, Cork. It has not been possible to ascertain which *Orkney Dawn* is in the photograph above.

Finvoy was purchased in 1957. She had been built in 1920 at Alloa for Belfast owners, and retained the same name throughout her life. On her third voyage for the company, her furnace crowns burnt out while on a voyage from the Humber to Kirkwall with barley. She was towed to Kirkwall and then to Aberdeen for repairs, but was there for some months due to a strike at the yard. She was sold in 1958 for scrapping at Irvine.

Steam came to an end in the South Isles with the withdrawal of *Orcadia* in 1958. *Hoy Head (II)*, formerly an Admiralty MFV built three years previously, which was chartered to Bremners by the Secretary of State for Scotland, replaced her. She was based at Longhope, sailing to Scapa on Mondays and Fridays, with calls at Lyness and Flotta, and to Stromness on Tuesdays, Wednesdays, and Saturdays, with additional calls on Hoy and at Graemsay. She is seen to the right here in a 1968 view at Stromness, with *Watchful* to the left. *Hoy Head (II)* was withdrawn in 1987 and was sold to Shetland owners who later sold her on.

Watchful was a similar vessel to *Hoy Head (II)*, built in 1944, and entered service in 1961. She was based at Stromness. In 1974 Bremners were taken over by the OISC, which were themselves taken over by Orkney Islands Council in 1987. *Watchful* was withdrawn from service in 1976.

From 1921 to 1928, the steamer *Countess Cadogan* offered a rival service to the South Isles. She had been built in 1897 by Bow McLachlan at Paisley for the Shannon Development Corporation for service on that river. In 1913 she had been sold for use on Lough Corrib, north of Galway. She was purchased in 1917 by N. Cook of Aberdeen, who had her rebuilt. She was operated from 1921 to 1924 by Captain Arcus, and from his death in the latter year to 1928 by James Sutherland, one of his crew. She was scrapped in 1932.

Robert Garden had been serving the Orkney Isles for five years with sail-powered floating shops, when he bought *Endeavour* in 1889. She sailed on a weekly circuit of the South Isles in that capacity from Scapa, and is seen here to the right, with *Hoy Head (I)* to the left. (*Alastair Cormack Collection*)

In 1913 *Endeavour* was fitted with a motor to replace her steam engine. She remained in service until 1928, was laid up and scrapped two years later. (*Alastair Cormack Collection*)

Cormorant had been built in 1885 and came into the ownership of Robert Garden in 1898. She was used to carry supplies to his shops on the west coast of Sutherland and as far south as Loch Broom. She was sold in 1934 to John R. Laird of Burray as relief steamer for *Sutors*, and was broken up there some four years later. (*Alastair Cormack Collection*)

Sutors, which had been built in 1913, was purchased in 1925 by Andrew Laird of Burray to serve that island. On Mondays she sailed to Scapa Pier for Kirkwall market day, and on Thursdays she sailed to St Margaret's Hope to connect with the weekly call of the North Company steamer. She served Burray until replaced by *Ailsa* in 1938. (*Alastair Cormack Collection*)

In 1938 John Laird purchased the steamer *Ailsa*, which had been built in 1906 by Ailsa Shipbuilding at Troon for the Girvan to Ailsa Craig service, and had been in service from 1924 on the Cromarty Firth. She was taken over by the Admiralty during the Second World War, and was used in the Normandy Landings. A few days after the end of the war the Churchill Barriers were opened, and Burray and South Ronaldsay were connected by road to the Mainland of Orkney.

A bow view of *Ailsa* in dock at an unidentified location, with a paddle steamer in the background.

The roll-on roll-off revolution also reached the South Isles. *Thorsvoe* was built in 1991 at Campbeltown for the South Isles service, which now started at Houton and served Lyness on Hoy and Flotta. She is now a reserve vessel. (*Craig Taylor, Alastair Cormack Collection*)

Hoy Head (III) (not illustrated) had been built in 1973 in the Faeroes as *Geira* for Shetland inter-island ferry services. She was purchased by the Orkney Islands Steamship Co. in 1987 and served the South Isles until 1994, when she was renamed *Hoy Head II* and sold to Kirkwall owners. *Hoy Head (IV)* (above) was built in 1994 at Bideford for the South Isles service. Lyness now has five sailings per day and Flotta four per day. (*Craig Taylor, Alastair Cormack Collection*)

Graemsay came in 1996 from the Ailsa yard at Troon, and is more of a passenger-cargo ferry with space for only one car. She serves Graemsay and Moaness on the north end of Hoy from Stromness. (*Craig Taylor, Alastair Cormack Collection*)

Graemsay in May 1999 at her berth in Stromness.